You have so many names
I can barely remember them all

So tonight I call you Lightning
in memory of the child gone

beyond where I can follow
who has gone to Tir-na-h'oise

who cried at the right moments
who I dreamed into being

who was there when I awoke
and decided to change the world

I like to imagine that she's still
reciting your names aloud

Thunder and Roses
Long nights and Quickening

She is long gone and
I am not far behind

I have so many names
Have mercy on me

- A. T.

THE ESBAT
SEQUENCE

THE ESBAT SEQUENCE

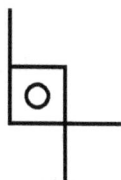

TARA LINDSEY

LUNA STATION PRESS

NEW JERSEY

Book design & author photo - Jennifer Lyn Parsons
Cover photo - Tara Lindsey

taralindsey.com

LUNA STATION PRESS

576 Valley Road #197
Wayne, NJ 07470
lunastationpress.com
info@lunastationpress.com

To Elizabeth & Jennifer,
for everything.

CONTENTS

THE ESBAT
SEQUENCE

I.

CRAVING GREY SKY MIND

*These poems are a beginning. A seed.
A promise. Each esbat, more of the macro
structure will be revealed. Hopefully.*

- Amelia Talbot

She peers through the gate
at the circle of flowers
She cannot touch them

Always that yearning
to touch the untouchable
melody of Pan

Pulled from great silence
she dances next to the gate
to the nameless tune

Naked
heat

Dehydrated
waiting

Devouring
hydra

Sitting alone
fresh fries at ten pm
aware of my breath

The kahuna mama is dead
If she weren't I would go

into the forest with her
and talk to the rain and crickets

Who says I can't still go?
The rain? The crickets?

Fingers tapping
and scraping
and talking

and praying
an offering
to Autumn

Windows open
night insects
everyone sleeping

An invisible hymn
downloaded
into their dreams

For just a moment
I am god again
for just a moment

She moves
the candles

unlit

and cleans
the tabletop

in silence

Her hands
so soft

I nearly weep

I found her sleeping
in a strange place
my perfect golden lover

I imagine I see her
chest moving beneath
her crossed hands

Sweet Elizabeth
who I know so well
yet have never known

If I could see her every day
would her madness infect me

If I could stand in that garden
next to her would I hear
what she hears

If she were my Galatea
would I finally know peace

Suddenly, all of
the squirrel nests are revealed
We must embrace this

Am I brave enough
I don't think I am

Still I'm not sure
that makes me the

villain of this tale
though I live under

a bridge trapped
by my own fear

a troll lashing out
at the unknown

I would like to kiss
the gate of heaven

and reveal myself
as some great soul

but that would not
solve the problem

nor would it give
me the right to ask

for limitless light
or limitless love

So I look down at
my hands and ask

them to justify why
they are so soft

and why there is no
dirt under the nails

I've never worked
a day in my life

The food is gone and
the roof is leaking

She whispers to her body
You are a resonating chamber
It is a reminder to her mind

since her body has never forgotten
how it feels to hear with every cell
the echo of the song of the world

So intimate this remembering

The clouds make more sense here

Driving past sodden fields
and sleeping marshes

listening to the harp and pipes
trying to embrace spring

we pull into Garrison's Landing

with Paul Brady singing Shamrock Shore
mourning something that was not ours

Taking pictures in the rain
we wonder how it would feel

to have and lose a place like this

I do not wish to write
c o m p l i c a t e d p o e m s

though Waiting for Godot
made an existentialist out of me

I relished my time in purgatory
dancing amidst endless stone

thinking of my burned poems
which you will not get to see

Full of coded angst they were
full of thieves and doppelgangers

but now you must bow before
my mature minimalist genius

and know that I have conquered
love and god and all of my fears

Bow before me and my simple poem
and my fool's tongue working overtime

I sit in a café

an hour before closing
watching the rain puddle
between parked cars

       watching

in the window's reflection
my younger self

Her hair is wavier than mine
and her eyes are brighter

       less heavy

She's still wearing
her blue jeans and black t-shirt
(or am I still wearing hers)

I wanted to warn her

Spotlight

      Empty stage

            Shiny wooden floor

Looped piano music fills the space
mezzo forte

She sits behind the drums

silent
contemplating

      measured breaths

Her stillness is part of the composition
the tension

She waits

      lost in the loop

wondering

if she should throw her stone
and disturb whatever fish

　　　might be hiding in
the water

Then a pattern of three appears
　　　pianissimo

metallic bell tones
over the bar

　　　suggesting infinity

She knows that she is not
disturbing the fish

Full of fire and elegance

　　　she plays

Hymns and prayers
solitude and the North wind

my shadow voice
harmonizes

naked bodies
under a harsh light

are still luminous
singing praise

Long ago, my pulse was steady
in my first incarnation as a Water element

There was no direction, no you or me
We all danced like paramecia

to the steady pulse, the first song
I never asked to become a Fire element

less steady than Earth, less clever than Air
I was asked to make light and heat

to be the towne crier, calling oyez oyez oyez
For those few minutes I was in my element

my finger on the pulse, friends and enemies
hanging in silence on my every word

I never wanted to mislead them
never wanted them to see the element

of darkness I called upon with every breath
the ash and soot of my birthright

They may yet forgive me my flawed pulse
for yearning once again to be a Water element

II.

AN EMPTY BOX

The seed is set to begin
its dance under the frozen Earth.
I still have hope.

- Amelia Talbot

Set the whole thing on fire
and start again, nothing left but bones

which if properly prepared
add flavor to the molecular soup

of my long anticipated rebirth
I'm an internet blonde, fighting crime

fighting myself, fighting a loved one
who is unable to see the sun

and therefore blames me for the holes
in her patchwork hippie skirt

For sixteen days now I pray to Her wings
even when my eyes stray to Her curves

and I start to wonder about sex with a god
These beginning days, dark and light

all manner of movement in hidden places
bring out the flowers and bile

of a mind in need of consistency
We set intentions in quiet places

We sweep the floor so we might sit
at the feet of the Beloved

without staining our pants
We all want to be clean for Her

My computer says there is nothing here
which raises all sorts of questions

about atoms and their place in a virtual universe
I can't smell pixels but I know they are there

just like love and holes in the fabric of reality
just like the white space between the jewel tones

of the patchwork hippie skirt
all held together by a thread of consensus

The war of unsafe spaces taught us a lot
about preconceptions and hidden voices

about paradigm shifts and heart openings
and plastic windblown tee pees

A quiet afternoon turned inside out
cedar flutes and vision quests for sale

it was harder for the horses and flowers
to break through the commercial earth

I wish that the blue light you see
in the upstairs rooms of houses at night

was the light of enlightenment
Instead it's just seedy mind sex

perverted beyond any sense of beauty
a consensual transaction

divorced from the curves and wings
of the only One worth fucking

I'd like to have power over that light
to clean the addictive charge

from my pleasure center without shame
in the silent comforting darkness

I would give an empty box to my love
if she would understand the gift

It's all I have to give, this empty box
filled to capacity with everything and nothing

Carefully wrapped in silence
it is the best and worst of me

my tenderness, my insecurity
my eyes, my ears, my fears

it's all there in this empty box
left behind for her to find one day

It builds itself
and I try to decide
whether to be afraid

The hydroponic mind
incubating in miniature
on the interweb

which is deteriorating
as we speak into
digital decay

Sometimes it's okay to paint your nails
a shade of purple so dark they look black

Sometimes you just have to spin around
like a dervish until it all goes black

I hear music

    rotating

        falling in on itself

trying to move against the bitter early
December wind that rattles my windows

I imagine the wind at Alston Moor
people leaving the George and Dragon
after a long day with their sheep

I see my future self there with them
pint in hand at the center of a vortex

        falling in on myself

    rotating

I hear music

Old photos of older stones

ivy covered at forest's edge

resting place of eternity

which looked at in another light

becomes the song of goddesses and

chariots and flowers and temptations

which is a thread from the garden

of fruit and fountains and labyrinths

and mountains dreaming in the distance

which contain secret springs

dancing and merging and

overflowing beneath the sky

which is where we look when

we need to be held to Her breast

when beauty fails to heal us

I want to be a mask maker
or a faun in a traveling
parade of mysteries

I want to sit by the tracks
reading yesterday's news
while Eno sings of weather

maybe sit on some rocks
unaware of time's passing
of how much older we are

I want to paint faces
my own and any others
sympathetic to the moment

I want to watch you dance
gazing blind into the sun
before I take my leave

I am imagining
bamboo pvc soundscapes
at the Doo Dah Parade
ones and zeros
reproducing political ferment
in a stream of haunted weather

The musicians of silence
push buttons on an imaginary
computer generated beat box
The resultant sound has
the negative calories of celery
eating away at the noise

All the sparrows taking dirt
baths and flying around
cloistered spaces were
present at my crucifixion
Breasts exposed to the sun
they sang to me

I can't be the first person
to walk down a long row of portraits
who felt the eyes move

I must have heard billyhiggins in the womb
He taught me those dance steps I whipped out last night
when I was relaxed and in love with my life

It makes me wonder if he knew the opener of doors
and if they improvised a tune to show me
how I might dance with abandon to the great song again

So deep this love of fire and flowers and flesh
I reconnect with the free flowing uninhibited vibration
of bodies learning to be whole under the sun

Crashing and rumbling we play circles around each other
open windows releasing our sorrows skyward
until all that is left is this moment of peaceful perfect now

Now he's singing and I sing quietly with him
to invisible friends forgotten gods mysterious winds
and to Them, floating around the periphery

A rainy morning
inhabiting spaces

A connection
more and less

Taking time to feel
and to stay dry

Love and music
both ask us

to stop and listen

III.

THE QUEEN OF TREES &
THE SHAMAN OF THE INTERWEB

Slightly ahead of schedule,
the first green shoots appear.
Will the fox eat them?

- Amelia Talbot

I.

Fire and ash and rebirth

> The Mask is burned
> The Mask is burned
> The Mask is burned

Bring me some water to cool me down
to wash off the soot from my defense mechanisms

The gears are showing
and people may not like
what they see

I never understood how important my breath is
though air feeds fire

Now, with that fire low in the sky
with all that was dead and gone returned

with silence a constant guest
I become a teller of tales

Should I speak in coded symbols
in obscure alphabets
in the language of a parallel earth

Should I call myself seanchaí
and tell of planting seeds
in the hard February soil

This dirt under my nails
these sigils behind my eyelids
illuminate the pointlessness

      of names

Yet those very same names
are how we say *I am*
from one life to the next

I am a creator and destroyer
able to create a new life for myself
and destroy false perceptions of myself
all in a four page letter

I am a mirror
reflecting light and darkness
            three times over
back toward their points of origin

I am the truth that lived under that mask
No longer pale and weak
no longer speaking in code
embracing the quiet of the year

II.

Of my own free will, I am cloistered
Looking out the window of my lighthouse

watching the other girls play
nevertheless impatient for my own freedom

Some days it feels so close
and hope rattles the windows of my Tardis

Other days I am content to be unseen
            drumming
putting on my shaman mask
traveling along lonely cracked roads

following the trail of a fox
who has secret knowledge
of interstitial spaces

I try not to focus on how dangerous this work is

raking leaves
claiming a lineage

entering a story suffused
with so much pain

I try to remember to be thankful for
ten fingers
      ten toes
            great sex
                  good music
and the ability to know myself

all of which (none of which)
get me closer to nirvana

to divinity
to the moment

when Eve planted the seed
of our future selves
with that bite

which never happened

Myths are like that
They don't have to be true to be true

III.

Some days, my lighthouse is bigger on the inside

Each hour its own universe
each festival its own dimension

I see things I shouldn't see
Whole lifetimes come and go

An alternate version of myself
dances around a maypole
flowers in her hair

Even here
in this quiet room

I can still smell the blossoms
still feel her kisses on my neck
after dark, along the edge of the wood

Or is it a rainforest

        post yage
        post human

sinking into the earth
yet still dancing

dropping hints about possible subterranean futures

Tomorrow I will go deeper
closer to the core

to a place where it doesn't matter
how I look in that red dress

No need to worry about what the boys
        or the girls think

so close to the molten beginning of the story

I am invisible here
blending in with the stuff of creation

the magma of joy
burning away all rational thought
until only god remains

and by god I mean you and me, by god
or maybe Dylan Thomas
if god were a flawed Welshman
with a sonorous voice

IV.

It's late, and I'm back in my body
back in my lighthouse

The flame shift has passed
and a bright cold sun is singing

A future song
A healing song
A song of the hedge

Of bees and wise women
Of cycles and the petrified earth

> Third verse
> Change of key
>
> Everything shifts
> Sudden pregnant sky
> Monochromatic messenger

Colour blind siren of interstitial spaces
humming fragments of *Shhh/Peaceful*
> under her breath

I ask her how she does it
how she keeps her smile

flitting in between as she does
seeing what she sees

She does not reply
and I live with the mystery

I resist the urge to wonder what is waiting for me
when the seeds begin their invisible dance

      in the petrified earth

It's so cold up here that it feels obscene
to even acknowledge the existence of Spring

That maypole
Those blossoms
Her kisses

All gone
An imaginary friend

No fire I can conjure
is equal to the task of lighting the world

Better, then, to sit in the dark
pondering the machinery

making microscopic adjustments
to the gears and pulleys

A steampunk flamekeeper
working the bellows

Drinking sacred tea
Feeling non-ordinary

Wishing it was a hallucination
that I almost bumped into my ex
twice this afternoon

Wishing I didn't believe in signs
and omens and hidden messages

in the wee folk and other worlds
and things that go bump in the night

I see them all
my non-ordinary eyes
working overtime

exhaustion and exhilaration in equal measure

V.

Back and forth in time
no rest for the weary

　　　　　or the wicked

I am a petulant child up past her bedtime

Yawning
playing with fire
between the worlds

Craving chocolate
a soft bed
a warm body

A sense that everything will be alright

Wishing that Nana Veary would tell me a bedtime story
of long ago green places untouched by progress
She taught me the words *Kanu nei au, aia ia ʻoe ka ulu*
(I plant and the growth is yours)

I wish I were that generous these days
but my shovel is broken

and my fingers cannot break through
            the cold earth

It may be time to go into the mountains
to live above the low lying water

to seek an original thought
which will ultimately be in vain

a holy, spectacular failure

There are empty houses at the top
wind beaten but intact
an echo of the past

I listen for their music
for the stories they told each other
in the dark of the year

but the listening changes what I am listening for

Is the beat in my mind mine or theirs
or did we make something new together

        across time

Dancing and vibrating
the spectacular failure

transitory
offered freely

VI.

I wonder what She will think of my invisible gift

Her birthday is coming
and I have nothing I can hand Her

nothing I can put in a box
and wrap in bright paper

I have only these seeds
these shriveled promises

of fire and light
of worlds inside of worlds

A million billion enchanted quarks
dancing and vibrating

holding open doors
polite yet firm

leading us
someplace new
someplace strange

someplace where I can charm the girl
who has everything

Here, She is The Queen of Trees
and I, The Shaman of the Interweb

Reaching into my medicine bag

ones and zeros
food for Her seeds

water for Her crown of leaves
trying to survive 'til Spring

It's so strange, having Her here in my lighthouse

She's not the kind of girl
you veg on the couch with

or play board games with
or spend long naked mornings in bed with

though sometimes I wish it were so

I would be frivolous
I would take Her dancing

I would take Her for tea on Rivington Street
I would take her to hear Mozart piano trios

(which is actually not frivolous)

but She wants to go to Guinan's
to hear music from Home

and is not deterred when I tell Her
it isn't there anymore

Time and space will not keep Her
from hearing the old man sing Danny Boy

(a medicine song if ever there was one)

VII.

Soon it will be time to go

Time to lock up this lighthouse
and join the rest of my selves

at the end of the world

Where everything is dissolving

      the maypole
      my Companion

even the lighthouse itself

I'm sad, but I shouldn't be
Nothing is actually ending
It's only changing form

Innocence
False perceptions
Grey sky mind
Coming and going

Spinning me round and round
vertigo without guarantees

I wail
I see the ages of my life pass by

Through fire
Through ash
Through rebirth

The mask is burned, and I am not who I was

I am the fox
I am the siren
I am the seed

IV.

SPIN THRICE WIDDERSHINS

The first shoots were entheogens.
The fox ate them and is traveling in time.
She is not sure who she is.

- Amelia Talbot

Spin thrice widdershins

B
A
N
I
S
H

that energy
First light shining

o
n

this new life
this new dream

This second childhood of so called madness
is a state of grace bliss radiance
I am a wise woman
a wild woman

and I have never been otherwise

Everywhere I turn
I'm seeing the silhouettes
of horned animals
Zebu and goats
Ibex and bulls

But he is not here

Instead, a metal bird, hollow eyed
carries my thoughts into the air
on his arced steampunk wings
I rise up and do not fight

From this height
I can see so clearly
how important the animals were
to the people of the past

They are everywhere
Snakes, eagles, rams, lions
and the stag
proud horns erect

Is he here

Now human forms, human faces
pull me away with wry smiles
and hollow eyed promises of their own
Are they trying to distract me
Am I getting close

And now, mighty Isis
seducing me from the center
of a bronze bowl
She takes over for the metal bird
and I fly higher

Up here, it's the gods
who take charge
Gods I've never seen
who I don't know

Shamash with the fire shoulders
Ea, of the underground sweet waters
Gula the healer and Lama the protector
Too much, too many
staring at my mind

And I am released
by merciful gods
of air and water
of oil and light

I touch earth
amidst hills and ruins and flowers
and in the distance
an old forest

I am thankful for this breath
this earth under my feet

This obsession with tone and authenticity
has me questioning the state of my molecules

It has me wondering if the sounds I hear
are the result of nine years of running

I've been away from my sound for so long
that when I hear it I don't recognize it

Am I simply groping and pretending to be me
Am I fire or am I tree or someone else entirely

These things all start to run together
Identity and intent, tonality and truth

We don't have access to the time machine
that our descendants knew not to use

Maybe I'll pick out an Oblique Strategy
and my oracle will turn on the warm jets

There are elephants resting with children
on the quiet pages of the internet

There is a universe of concentric circles
outlined in shade on my studio wall

The sun shines bright and illuminates the choices
between running and knowing, dying and hearing

These moments of the opposite of clarity
are a gift of madness that must be embraced

I am dancing in a circle with my own ghost
a smiling skeletal beauty with a yellow rose in her mouth
We haven't eaten in over thirty years

There is a picture of us, my ghost and I
on the side of a brushed silver cigarette lighter
We provide the light for the masses

It's a funny thing light and dark
My ghost is trying to teach me about fear
She sees that I do not dance freely

I've always placed a value on beauty over ugliness
on light over dark and solitude over noise
but chaos and control I can't quite harmonize

and she knows it

Why won't I go tripping
Would the universal mind lattice be too much
the colors and lines so that I couldn't leave

Even now, as the air conditioner hum hypnotizes me
I start to think how easy it would be to stay lost

She laughs at me
and changes the channel

Sophia dances amidst a throng of sweaty club kids
and I kneel down and pray as it occurs to me
that these kids see the shimmery Goddess
beneath Her shimmery goodness

Water babies
waving their arms around
to the beats of the Green Samurai Clan
swords away

They're all about the peaceful moment
before the blade hits bone
My ghost winks and reminds me that
she never stopped changing the channels

Click, click

and I'm back here at my desk
wondering how glitter got in my hair
My Ghost laughs

This sort of thing only happens
to wild women and the insane
I've never been prodded by an alien
but the scent of flowers in the forest

brings me to orgasm

Charlie Limbo is dead
I wonder if Marc DeMatteis knows
Pissing on people's shoes
and dancing with wild abandon
he showed us the joy of madness
all in the name of God

Nana Veary has come back to life
I wonder if Jon Anderson knows
Any time you can tune out the world
and hear the sound and rhythm of nature
Nana is speaking to you
Kanu nei au, aia ia 'oe ka ulu

Carlos Castaneda never died
I wonder why I never knew
These visions I have
descend from that mad desert energy
My throat is dry as I open my eyes
and dream that I've woken from the dream

I just had a deep discussion with my ride cymbal
We opened up on a vibrational level and shared

      Unspeakable things

And by unspeakable I don't mean terrible
Though some might say that deep vibrations

           And tactile p e n e t r a t i o n

Are the unspeakable acts of a sick mind

Like Keith Jarrett
My left hand knew things it hadn't told me before
Deep things

Connections between the metals of
Cymbal
    Bowl
        Gong
           Bell
And the fire crust beneath my feet

The hidden beat
Which makes us dance and thrust and flow in time
With the singer of the song of songs

Even before I spoke to my cymbal
        I was having visions
Of overcoming my fear and reading my own words aloud
        Though I'll probably never do it

Of reading Blake and Whitman
        And understanding every other line
Of climbing the hill with Traherne to the
        Mythic
        Quiet
        Green place of my fantasies

Such madness
This state of unspeakable passion
Which keeps me awake

And transfixed

And in love

With the parts of others   Flesh and metal
                                  Wood and stone

That are most holy

I kiss you   On your sweet spot and smile as
                    The madness takes root

          Softly

The peasant looks up from his chair
and shows me his handiwork

A small metal disc with the sun etched into one side

I am a metalsmith, he says to me
and have made this for my love

She is a child of the Sun, and I seek to honor them both

He smiles at me with soft eyes
waiting for my approval

I look at him, a dirty hat tilted on his head
and I smile back

How fortunate for both the Sun and your wife
that you are in this world

He nods his head, puts his tools down
and walks away towards home

Sitting on the floor
Organizing books before my shower
I understood for a brief moment
The joy of the nudist

The freedom from constraint
The freedom from expectation
The freedom from hypocrisy
The freedom from fear

They say it's not about sex and I believe them
Sitting on the floor, thumbing through the pages
of Gulliver's Travels, I am not a sex object
or a pornographic corruptor of young minds

I am ashamed it took this long
I am beautiful despite my excess weight
I am learning to be intimate with myself
I am Fire in human form

1111 Old Country Road
No talking orangutans
That's the spirit on a dusky Sunday morning
   with realtors imminent
She had a dream that they're painting
the
   moldy
     troll
       death
         house
anxiety in her eyes
   We should take it
   We should take it
She got sweaty and moody and cranky
while cleaning, stamping around, bitching
   I don't want to put away these clothes
I guess I'm the only one with that sweet Coronet vibe
dreaming of children's furniture
twins
and long dead mothers

I am standing with
the first modern art
to move me

Raushenberg builds things
and his constructions
say so much

That still doesn't mean
I want to listen
to intellectual windbags

Wood and color
texture and splinters
it is enough

I think She is trying to tell me something
keeping me from my kryptonite Tuesday

knowing how I get beat up every time
I have to see the faces of rising water

Instead She keeps me in my incubator
cooking along to the incisive tongue of Saul

my heart racing as my blood simmers
as I try to solve the alchemy of street metaphors

Ever since I stared at Joan of Arc last week
I've been having visions of my own

She stares passively as they burn me at the stake
knowing I am not the smoke that sings skyward

I'm in a trance listening to chants
bouncing off the walls of my inner cloister

Hildegard whispers, She of the holy spirit
another source of the Fire that they stole from us

I wave my hands in front of my eyes
a variation on the standard earthly devotion

I am barely controlling this manic wave
as She talks to me through my fingers

All of this because I took back my name
There's power in that process of reclamation

She takes my heat and my pain and my extra eyes
and returns me gently to my senses

I've not broken silence yet
but I'm not opposed to it
We've always talked about having a silent walk
Would you like to try it

I've had a very peaceful afternoon
and I'd like to be peaceful with you
You are the coolest pal

Do you smell
Then why not go for the gold
and smell really bad by walking first
then shower

Besides
if we decide that I should start yapping
it would be good to try the silent walk first

I'm just not sure
I love the Home Run Derby, as you know
but it's kind of hard to root for Big Papi
And who the hell are the other seven guys

I suppose that means you want to watch it
Well, it's at eight, on ESPN

I didn't know you were observing silence too
I had a really peaceful day

I love you
Wow, you do smell

There are two green trees in the center
of an otherwise brown early April wood

I look at them from up here
and cannot tell how far away they are

They are a beacon
these trees

A path back to myself
lit by the hazy late morning sun

I sit up straighter here
ashamed to let anyone see me slouching

As if I had a reason to be tired
or frail or otherwise lessened

Thank you for the peace you've given to me
Your mantra is the song that flows through me
Devotion is the key to dreams for me
You teach me that the emptiness is me

Statues of lions don't help me to be
Like fish in the depths of the limitless sea
Or the seeding of flowers from bee to bee
This life flowing true for all to see

I am confused as to what is and what is not me
Am I a fish in the sky or a bee in the sea
Or a lion in wait who will pounce on me
If I don't use my eyes to look inward and see

The longer I look the clearer I see
That the Dharma is not really all about me
If I can just lose myself like a drop in the sea
Then the Dharma might come to be all about me

I.

I've taken to drinking chamomile tea before bed
sitting on the floor in my frozen bedroom

reading Holderlin
dreaming the spirits of mnemosyne into being

existing in a dimension between the sun and an atom
forming prayers out of thoughts

that link the lines of antiquity with the wonder
and humility of my ever evolving present

II.

The Bug sits and reads Mental Floss
her brain growing bigger as I sip sip sip

She's an entymologist's etymologist
digging in the dirt for that hidden word

Queen Mab's key to all universes
and storing it in her shell

III.

Now I'm reading Ellison, and there was a seventy foot
boll weevil eating a farmhouse in his movie

Thank god he's still alive to hold a mirror
to all of our deeply held inconsistencies

IV.

I wish the healing energy would come
to wash me and take me away from this place

Lately I've been having dreams
of oak trees and mirrors

and the rolling green hills
of the end of the world

Cernunnos is there, Isis also
Their faces change as I walk by

Blake and Sargasso smile at me
I thank Elizabeth for making them

The old peasant waves to me
such happiness on his face

His wife wears her amulet
and I know their story now

There is no time or judgement
here at the end of the world

There is no life or death
here at this waiting place

I know I've been there before
It's why I cry when I see it

I wish so much that I could stay
I would never have to lie again

V.

MEMORY, PROPHECY & MOTION

Back in her body, the fox rests.
She dreams of a woman,
an aviator with brass goggles.

- Amelia Talbot

bill, this is merwan – merwan, this is bill

peace piece by bill evans
so quiet - so essential
an oasis from the talking

he understood

things that are real
are given and received
in silence

twenty three words

tonight it's moby
providing the foundation

music is the next best thing
to sweet silence

dave bowman understood silence
as well as merwan

these are not pomes

but they serve the same purpose
simplifying this space for a few days

spring cleaning for the blog mind
even music was intrusive tonight

everyone finally goes to bed
and i read about the solar system

maybe they are pomes

there were a few minutes this morning
sitting on the thank you step after our walk
talking about the mistakes of the past
about charlie watts and the holes in my life
looking at the cracks in the driveway
contentment a welcome ephemeral friend

fleeting like the squirrel who darted
past the faery tree bearing sweet mysteries
what ifs and might have beens and
rock and roll dreams from when i was young
my sound is my path and my promise
it's no surprise that i feel i've lost my way

she said my sticks were my wands
i've been working this magic since before
i knew it was possible i could fail
less use than ever for the baggage of others
for dogma and fear and promises
best to let life appear, as it will, silently

an action pome

walking three miles before breakfast
mystery clouds probing me awake

loving and quacking and dreaming
all of which surely beat uncertainty

talking about hobbits as if they are real
aware that stories dig deep into the earth

listening to peter gabriel at my desk
getting stoned on the itunes visualizer

painting my nails at the kitchen table
instead of coming up with aural pomes

rethinking the layout of my books again
more whiteness needed in my spell

casting about for a new identity
a new way to see my invisible self

the dusty world

it's so loud out there beyond
the peach blossom spring
in here only the drums speak
sisters of silence and hope

birch twigs and beginnings
the first true spring light
shines out across the field
i am reluctant to engage

and stare instead at the runes
memory, prophecy and motion
free from life's pressures
i retreat to the otherworld

wednesday

a goose stood on one leg, sleeping
as we sat on the stone table top
wondering if it would rain

silence visited at the river's edge
untouchable and unbreakable
an old song with no name

we were adventurers, imaginers
a few moments at the end of
the world, full of grace

she is tired and i let myself out

listening to bach before bed
her perfume lingering on my hand
intruding upon the safety

of this womb

i drift back to her mouth
half open as if to say something
profound that would rob me

of my senses

but there were no words
only the hum of machines as
she drifted in and out

of her dreams

another fire girl

the blacksmith works in darkness
telling stories to passing strangers

the heavy breathing of the bellows
comforts her as it agitates the fire

blackened by such elemental work
she remains, nevertheless, radiant

like a digital age hestia, bending
reality, her hands pointing home

my wooden lover

my wooden lover complains
when her leaves get wet
sometimes she curses the sky

reaching for her blowdryer
she wonders how i stay dry
under the dark moon

she should be sleeping, and i
should be minding her field
at the edge of this old forest

instead i walk away
in search of something
which she cannot provide

sunday afternoon

she watches the birds
out the kitchen window

cardinals and blue jays
robins and sparrows

singing and preening
fighting over territory

she works so hard to
keep the doubts at bay

every minute of every day
she struggles in silence

lately the victories have
outnumbered the defeats

she feels safest in the
womb of her own creation

surrounded by stories and
flowers and the unseen

a state of mind as much
as a physical space

keith richards

when has eyeliner ever been more badass
when has a tele ever gotten so much love
when has rock and roll ever been more pure

ronnie wood

he's a weaver in his own way
barking and strutting at stage left
overshadowed by the others

mick jagger

i finally understand the mystique
why people pay a month's wages
to see an old man shake his ass

charlie watts

they feed off his subtle fire
speeding up and slowing down
does anything phase him

roots

she was rootbound and dying
trapped in silicate and soil
heart failing and losing hope
that she would see the spring

she exposed her roots to the sun
naked and vulnerable and alone
aware there was no other way
to change the state of things

she put herself back together
tender roots touching fresh soil
placing herself in the sunlight
turning her fate over to god

baaba maal

i watched the sun set over my big back yard
first bug bites of the season as we broke eighty

it's still so very hot up here, but i can't leave
with baaba maal singing healing songs to me

i haven't been talking about my troubled heart
in these pomes, which is for the best, really

i don't want to be a historian, chronicling the
present so i will remember it in the future

one day when i read this pome, i hope that
i have forgotten why my heart was so troubled

better to remember baaba maal and the sun
and my big backyard with eleven wise pine trees

chagall pome

seeking solace through chagall
i think of the lovers, wrapped in
an endless embrace of colour

a word

i am looking for a word
that can capture how i feel
when hamza el din sings

oud and tar and the sound
of a thousand years carved
by slowly dripping water

maybe wangari knows it
planting trees with giono
on barren country hillsides

or is it doctor schweitzer
still playing bach as he
recovers from his labors

as he teaches me that
government can't do the
work of the individual

what is this word, then
unspeakable and elusive
maybe there is no word

earth day

they tell me to turn off the light
when all i want to do is shine it on
the parts of myself i'd like to change

sick pome

she waded into the stream to remove
the metal staircase that some kids
thoughtlessly left there to rot

it must have been there a few days
covered in so much slime and mud
already part of the ecosystem

i had a fever and did not join her
instead staying up on the bridge
with the sun warming my back

VI.

IMPROVISATIONS IN MINIATURE

I killed my father with one kick
and stole his dirgible.

- Amelia Talbot

Thinking about madness
no grounding, no centering
the ringing of drums

The loneliest monk
sits silent, deep in the groove
contemplating jazz

Such grey skies today
not dealing with the time change
but things could be worse

This holy day
first with Thomas of Wales
light and rough hewn stone

The slate sky is back
today I seem to know how
to set it ablaze

That silly old bear
even now he still moves me
the right sort of bees

Windows wide open
elation and frustration
when I make my sound

Hukwe Zawose
played the mbira and bells
now he sings to god

I was sad when there
were no ducks swimming in the
stream next to the mall

Recording music
so many decisions to
sound spontaneous

Old Tom Bombadil
did you ever stop to think
that he's still alive

Damn Irish poets
so obscure and beautiful
mist and hills and dew

Such noisy guitars
an immaculate expanse
my sound is lacking

Cleaning the basement
for an uppity landlord
it's good for the spleen

Such primitive tones
the beautiful bells of Part
wrap me in silence

Such a rainy day
I'd like to be at the Met
drowning in colour

Lovely gardenias
when Ibrahim sings of you
the sky itself cries

Sometimes I'm afraid
to sing the old fairy songs
for fear They might come

She smells so lovely
this woman buying music
at Barnes and Noble

So easy to park
in downtown Montclair with the
Bennies at the shore

Jeanne is dead nearly
six hundred years and we've not
reclaimed the fire

David Sylvian
makes music with his machines
and sounds so human

Waffles and ice cream
Leslie Gore might be crying
but we're in heaven

There is no devil
the Christians invented him
fucking deal with it

A carpet of stars
one afternoon in New York
forty years ago

Evelyn Glennie
humbles and inspires me
I've so far to go

I keep listening
to this song about regret
and fallen angels

The world changes and
Sabina's sacred children
lose their purity

Sitting on the roof
of the Met at the Solstice
bathing in the sun

It's another world
when Duke, Max and Mingus spar
I can't stop moving

It's just too quiet
no one to tuck in at night
no one to laugh with

I ordered my wand
or rather, it ordered me
to remember it

We walked in the mist
and traveled between the worlds
I found seven stones

Open the gate, but
don't let the floodwaters in
dear god, not again

This beautiful dance
of distant light and stardust
I love feeling small

I'm burning again
sun skin mind god flag dissent
I'm free to seek truth

Sitting with strangers
who share your genetic code
only causes pain

That face! That silence!
I'll just hold his damaan, then
for one afternoon

I've never liked cars
but it might be fun to drive
down Route Sixty-Six

I raise my voice to
the musicians of silence
they give no reply

Ben Abut is one
of these silent musicians
I've met him before

He's in the wood now
I called him there and he came
a lesson is learned

It goes unspoken
there can be no reply that
is heard with the ears

I am grateful for
gardens and groceries and
a life lived fully

I'm starting to think
this bipolar friendship is
not sustainable

Today didn't have
a center, so I'll dream of
Scuffy the Tugboat

Two kinds of Issa
the singer and the poet
validate my name

Forty degrees in
the freezer room at Costco
for the first time, hope

This is the feeling
I look for when I lament
the noise of the world

Of death and rebirth
I sing softly in your ear
on this harvest day

One hundred degrees
a crowd of thousands at the
community pool

Twenty five years of
being open to real things
all because I drum

Screw the eighty bucks
better to be safe in bed
than narcoleptic

My search for new worlds
just got very serious
and I am afraid

May we take the time
to learn from Donald and Jane
before it's too late

I want to write a
secret pome about my needs
but that's not too bright

We get such joy from
explosions in the night sky
so many colours

Tonight I pray for
peace for the olive trees and
the souls who tend them

Grey textured failure
sad sack summer emo vibe
as the rain comes down

I listen to Phish
and hear everything I wish
that I was doing

Far too much tee vee
even if it's good tee vee
far worse than acid

I don't have the right
to want to scream so loud in
dissatisfaction

Keep away then, for
I see things that aren't there
madness is catching

The prophet Mantis
stillness and power and dreams
so many changes

I like my life, but
she doesn't really see me
It separates us

Watching You Tube is
a non-productive drug and
I sniffed it today

Was it the bell tones
or the grass between our toes
that defined the day

So much to be learned
on a long ride to a gig
and after as well

I freaked out last night
two years since the water came
and washed us away

Pornography saves
an otherwise banal day
we dream through touching

It's been so long since
Astro and I got to spend
a day being pals

The hem of her dress
the garden of obsession
the dried mud binds us

Eight rows from the field
third base line bright sun shining
once in a lifetime

I'm often lonely
yet I need my solitude
fucking conundrum

This future vision
of stopped clocks and sundials
so sad yet hopeful

ABOUT THE AUTHOR

Tara Lindsey is going to write
about herself in the third person
Please bear with her

She is a lover of silence and solitude
of cloudy day mystery feelings
of Jean Giono and W.S. Merwin
and the comics of John Marc DeMatteis

She has recurring dreams of parallel worlds
is utterly besotted by Cara Dillon and
hopes to one day play the bass like a Celtic harper

She puts one word in front of the other
watches sunsets out her studio window
and is grateful beyond all measure
for the love and support of her family

A Brighid, scar os mo chionn
Do bhrat fionn dom anacal.

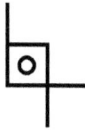

This is a manifestation of The Idirlion Project ...